DIGITAL PLAYGROUNDS

Our Kids & Video Games

AMANDA FAROUGH AND RACHEL KOWERT, PHD

Carnegie Mellon University: ETC Press
Pittsburgh, PA

CONTENTS

Kids love to play. Play is an integral part of childhood for a reason; children learn profound skills through play. Video games are ubiquitous in both our culture and, in many cases, our classrooms. The days of putting our collective heads in the sand about video games are over.

Fortunately, you're not alone. We're here to help you navigate these digital waters together.

First, we have Dr. Rachel Kowert. She's a research psychologist and mom of three. Rachel has been studying the uses and effects of games for more than 10 years with a specific focus on the ways games impact us physically, socially, and psychologically. She's published a variety of books and scientific articles relating to the psychology of games and also hosts a YouTube channel Psychgeist (www.youtube.com/psychgeist) which serves to bridge the gap between moral panic and scientific knowledge on a variety of psychology and game related topics.

There's also Amanda Farough (not a doctor). Amanda's been many things in her life — business analyst, consultant, game journalist, speaker, entrepreneur, and writer. Over the course of her work as an analyst and journalist, she's focused on the business side of how video games are made (www.virtualeconcast.com) and on how parents can navigate the world of games without being gamers themselves. Amanda has four kids and when she's not writing, streaming (www.twitch.tv/readyplayermama), or consulting on video games, she's hanging out with them.

Between the two of us, we're going to lead you through the world of video games as parents. It can be a little scary and definitely a bit (okay, a lot) intimidating, but once you have the language and the context to navigate these conversations with your kids, you'll be a pro before you know it. You might not be a Fortnite pro, but you will definitely be better equipped to talk to your kid about it.

So, let's start at the basics. At its core, games are playful experiences and we aim to start with defining what play really is.

WHAT IS PLAY?

Play is an activity unique from all others as it stands 'consciously outside ordinary life'[1]. It's an activity that completely absorbs us, is not associated with any material interest or profit, and exists within its own boundaries of space and time. While play can vary in terms of its style, from structured activities with explicit rules (e.g., games) to unstructured and spontaneous activities (e.g., playfulness), all forms of play share the qualities of being elective (i.e., you choose to freely engage in them) immersive, and are distinctly separate from the traditional routines of life.

Play Is What We Do When No One Is Looking.

As humans, we have been playing since the beginning of time. Archaeologists have found old ruined cities with card decks and dice uncovered within. Play has always been an integral component of human life throughout the lifespan and particularly critical for child development. Through play, kids learn about the world and themselves. They also learn a variety of life skills, like being more confident and engaging in creative thinking. On top of all of that, playing provides a variety of mental health benefits, including reduced stress and depression. Play's important element of creating and maintaining friendships, but we'll get more into that in the second book of this series.

To better understand some of the complexities of play, researchers in the mid-twentieth century identified four different styles of play: Agon, Alea, Mimicry, and Ilinx[2].

Agon refers to competitive play that you would find in classic games such as Chess or Checkers. Alea refers to chance-based games, like slot machines or lottery play. Mimicry refers to role playing; that is, assuming the role of a character and progressing through a story. Ilinx refers to play that alters one's perceptions, such as racing downhill.

While some activities incorporate only a single form of play other playful activities can incorporate a variety of elements. For example, collective card games (such as *Magic: The Gathering*) combine Alea (through the random shuffling of the cards), Agon (through competition) and Mimicry (as the cards represent imaginary constructs controlled by the player) play types.

If you took a moment to think about some of your favorite digital games, you would quickly see that many of them also combine play types. For example, in *Witcher 3* (CD Projekt Red), a role-playing game, the player engages in mimicry (through the narrative storyline) as well as elements of Alea (randomized reward drops) and Agon (as the player determines the best strategy for which of the side quests they should embark on). Within the game itself there is also a competitive, collectible card game called *Gwent* that also incorporates different elements of play, including Agon and Alea.

Purpose Of Play

Take a trip back with us to your own childhood for a moment. Regardless of the expression of play for you — sports, toys, pretend, school games on the playground — your time playing had a purpose. You were learning new social, motor, and cognitive skills that would become integral to your understanding of the world around you.

While play is inherently frivolous in nature (i.e., "it exists outside our daily activities"), it serves several purposes including social connection, mood management, and learning.

Social connection

Games provide a space for people to connect on a different level than socializing alone. Playing together with others allows us to offer and receive various levels of "social currency". First, social currency. Games provide a space where we can socialize about the game itself but can also serve as a springboard for broader discussions about ourselves and our lives. Second, emotional currency. Games, especially ones that allow for role playing, can provide a safe arena to explore topics that may be difficult to discuss without the added distraction of the game. For example, co-playing *Final Fantasy 7* (Square Enix) and collectively experiencing the loss of Aerith (one of the game's characters) in a room full of your friends provides a unique opportunity to discuss shared experiences and emotions around grief and loss. Lastly, tangible favors. Nothing helps solidify a friendship like a friend choosing to not attack and kill your character in a friendly game of *Dungeon Mayhem* (Wizards of the Coast) or accuse you of murder in *Clue* (Hasbro).

Research supports this idea as well as friendships have been found to be "emotionally jump started" in games. That is, trust is established much sooner with friends who play games together because you quickly learn who you can trust... and who you cannot. This has been found to lead to the development of close, intimate friendship bonds[3]. This is specifically the case in online games, as a considerable amount of research has found that friendships formed in these spaces are close, meaningful, and long-lasting.

Up to 75% of online game players report making "good friends" within their gaming communities. Of those, between 40%[4] and 70%[5] report regularly discussing offline issues with their online friends, including concerns they have not yet discussed with their offline friends. In other words, people not only view the relationships they form in online games as meaningful, but online gaming spaces are providing a method of communicating important personal topics with others.

Games provide the opportunity to strengthen and maintain friendships in a multi-faceted way because of their integration of playfulness and opportunities for collaboration and (hopefully, friendly) competition.

Mood management

Research has found that games are effective vehicles for reducing stress and helping manage one's mood (mood management) in a variety of ways. Specifically, there is quite a bit of research looking at how media and entertainment in general contributes to mood management and repair. Entertainment media is an efficient coping strategy to bring negative emotions and mood back into balance. For example, bored individuals choose exciting TV programs to watch whereas stressed individuals prefer to watch relaxing TV programs[6]. So if you're bored, you're going to potentially opt for a binge session of a show like The Witcher (Netflix). If you're feeling life nipping at your heels a little too hard, you're likely going to want the decidedly more mellow vibes of Ted Lasso (Apple TV+).

Games are particularly effective tools for mood management, because good games are developed to be engaging in a way that meets all of our basic psychological needs as humans: autonomy, competence, and relatedness[7]. Games give us a sense of autonomy (freedom to make your own choices), competence (achieve things, be successful), and relatedness (connecting with the other players and friends via online play). These three components – autonomy, competence and control – are universal and essential for psychological health and well-being of an individual.

This idea is referred to as Self Determination Theory or SDT. SDT was originally the "theory of motivation" during the 1970s. It's recently been expanded upon to talk specifically about games and how well-designed games can contribute to our well-being, in addition to a sense of happiness and satisfaction[8]. Having these needs met, while also having the added element of playfulness, is a pleasant feeling that makes us feel happy and satisfied.

Learning

Games have long been utilized in educational spaces as vehicles for learning. This is because they are incredibly effective at holding a player's attention while conveying information.

However, when it comes to games and learning the image that pops into mind is *Math Blaster* from the late 1980s, early 1990s. Equations flew across a screen that you had to "blast" by solving for "X". It wasn't nearly as engaging as the games of today. However, our understanding of how games can be vehicles for learning has come a long way since then, and we now understand that well-designed games can teach us a whole lot... even when they are not designed for that purpose specifically.

Some more modern examples of learning games are *Adventure Academy*, *Go Noodle*, *Prodigy Math*, *Camp Wonderopolis*, *Toca Labs*, *iCivics*, and *National Geographic Kids*.

Video games are great vehicles for learning because they induce a state of flow[9]. Often referred to as being "in the zone", players experience flow states when in-game challenges are balanced with the skill level of the player.

When in a state of flow, players become hyper focused on the in-game task and are determined to complete them because their skills are being challenged. It is in this state that various kinds of learning can occur. Games are also great vehicles for learning because people want to play them. In this sense, video games are ideal learning tools: people want to play them, they are fun, and flow enhances learning.

Research has found games to "unintentionally" teach a variety of skills and abilities including creative thinking[10], problem solving, time management, and leadership skills[11].

Leadership skills are also often discussed in the context of unintentional learning as they can be developed and played in online games, as Amanda describes below. Online games provide a particularly unique opportunity to observe, learn, and lead groups of all sizes, ages, and backgrounds. Experimenting with, and experiencing success in, leadership roles online have been found to cross over into other offline contexts.

One of the things that Amanda learned through her time playing massively multiplayer online games (MMOs, as defined in a later section) with her dad and future husband was how to work well with a team that you knew (family) and didn't know (newer guildmates). But unlike doing group work in school, this kind of collaboration was deeper and much more intimate. Everyone had a part to play in a dungeon or raid and everyone helped each other to reach the guild's goals. She learned the elements of great teamwork and compassionate leadership through video games over the many years that she played MMOs.

Players can also unintentionally pick up a new range of knowledge while playing video games, the nature of which depends on the video game they are playing. For example, you can learn about history by playing games like *Age of Empires* or what it takes to be a successful city planner by playing the popular simulation series *SimCity* (Electronic Arts) — or even *Cities: Skylines* (Paradox Interactive) for those that want even more granular control. Or, for those that relish the wonders of the world, key world leaders, and world history, there's the glory of the *Civilization* series (Take-Two, Firaxis).

All that learning that you did through playing with other children and on your own wasn't necessarily to escape the world around you. Playing (as children and as adults) is an augment — an opportunity to inject creativity and imagination into the moments between responsibilities and checkboxes. It's an important demarcation point that allows us to be light and free, even when the world feels heavy.

Now that we understand what play is and how we use it to navigate the world around us, we need to dive into the dialectical differences between analog play and digital play.

1. Huizinga, J. (1949). Homo Ludens. London: Routledge & Kegan Paul Ltd.

2. Caillois, R. (1958). Man, Play, and Games. Paris: Gallimard Education.

3. Yee, N. (2002). Befriending Ogres and Wood-Elves -Understanding Relationship Formation in MMORPGs. nickyee.com. Retrieved November 25, 2009, from http://www.nickyee.com/hub/relationships/home.html

4. Cole, H. & Griffiths, M. (2007). Social interactions in massively multiplayer online role-playing gamers. Cyberpsychology, Behavior, and Social Networking, 10(4), 575-583.

5. Williams, D., Ducheneaut, N., Xiong, L., Zhang, Y., Yee, N., & Nickell, E. (2006). From Tree House to Barracks: The Social Life of

Guilds in World of Warcraft. Games and Culture: A Journal of Interactive Media, 1(4), 338–361.

6. Bryant, J., & Zillmann, D. (1983). Using television to alleviate boredom and stress: Selective exposure as a function of induced excitational states. Journal of Broadcasting, 28(1), 1- 20.

7. Deci, E. L., & Ryan, R. M. (2008). Self-determination theory: A macrotheory of human motivation, development, and health. Canadian psychology/Psychologie canadienne, 49(3), 182.

8.   Ryan, R. M., Rigby, C. S., & Przybylski, A. (2006). The motivational pull of video games: A self-determination theory approach. Motivation and emotion, 30(4), 344-360.

9. Cowley, B., Charles, D., Black, M., & Hickey, R. (2008). Toward an understanding of flow in video games. Computers in Entertainment (CIE), 6(2), 1-27.

10. Bowman, N. D., Kowert, R., & Ferguson, C. J. (2015). The impact of video game play on human (and orc) creativity. In Video games and creativity (pp. 39-60). Academic Press.

11. Sherry, J. (2015). Debating how to learn from video games. In R. Kowert & T. Quandt (Eds.), The Video Game Debate, (p. 116-130). New York: Routledge.

THE RISE OF DIGITAL PLAY

While it is easy to categorize board games and even imaginary play as "play", digital play has somehow come to be categorized in its own separate box. We are very quick to understand the importance of learning to strategize during a game of Chess, pretending to be an adult in a profession of our choosing (Rachel played "school" a lot and Amanda was more prone to "house"), or engaging in a neighborhood game of tag.

However, digital play is often seen as somehow separate from traditional forms of play, despite being fueled by the same mechanisms. Even though the mediums of play are different — analog versus digital — the expression of play is remarkably similar.

Before we get to what games look like today, we need to dive into what games were like in the Days of Yore. The way that video games were made, discussed, and even regulated looked a lot different before the end of the 20th century.

The first commercial arcade video game was *Computer Space*, released in 1971. The game itself isn't widely known today, but we would be hard pressed to find someone who does not know the joy of the dimly lit auras of arcade parlors. As arcades enjoy a more recent resurgence, even our kids are getting a taste of what it was like in those early days of gaming. Arcades first became popularized in the late 1970s as spaces for fun, entertainment, and social connection. *Pong* (1972), *Night Driver* (1976), *Death Race* (1976) and *Space Wars* (1977) are some particularly notable titles.

In the 1980s, home consoles started to emerge. The Atari (and subsequent Atari 2600) were the first consoles to become both recognizable and popular, though certainly not by today's standards. Some of the most recognizable digital game titles first emerged in this era, including *Pac-Man* (1980), *Donkey Kong* (1982), *The Legend of Zelda* (1986), and the first of many *Mario Bros.* (1983) games. In the 1990s, we saw the concurrent rise of console and computer titles, including the first iteration of *Super Mario Kart* (1992), *Doom* (1993), and *Quake* (1996).

Alongside the big titles of the moment, educational games were a mainstay for '90s kids with computer labs in their elementary schools. Educational games like *The Oregon Trail* (1971), *Math Blaster* (1985), *Reader Rabbit* (1986), and even *Microsoft Encarta* (1995) blurred the lines between education and entertainment in a way that many children would never have experienced before. Edutainment exists today, of course, especially as mobile apps and websites that teachers use in their classrooms. Educational games in the '80s and '90s walked so that modern edutainment could run.

While the kids were getting dysentery and blasting aliens with math equations, developers were starting to experiment with higher fidelity graphics and different kinds of games. Developers moved from floppy disks to CD-ROM and console cartridges and the games became bigger and much more immersive. With technological constraints loosening every year, developers like id Software began releasing the first FPS (first-person shooter) games like *Doom*, *Wolfenstein*, and *Quake*. NetherRealm introduced '90s gamers to the most sophisticated fighting game of its time, *Mortal Kombat*. But with these violent games making their way into children's hands, parents were starting to sit up and notice that games weren't toys and certainly weren't just for children.

The game industry was faced with regulation from the government (and not just in America) without context and understanding of the industry at large. In 1993, the United States Congress held hearings about what to do about "realistic depictions of violence" in video games. At the time, individual consoles were responsible for classifying ratings for their games, which meant that what was considered "mature" on Sega Genesis wasn't regulated at all on the Super Nintendo platform.

The United States Congress introduced the Video Games Rating Act of 1994, which created all kinds of internal panic at game studios around the country. Congress was standing firm. It was either game studios figure out how to regulate video game ratings in the US or the government would do it. As a result, the biggest developers and publishers in the United States came together to form the Interactive Digital Software Association (IDSA) in April 1994. In November 1994, the IDSA (which would be renamed to the Entertainment Software Association in 2003) established the Entertainment Software Ratings Board (ESRB). The goal was to help consumers better understand the appropriateness of the content in video games and to ameliorate Congress' skittishness around video games in general.

As of 2022, the ESRB has established the ratings as follows[1]:

- E (Everyone)
- E10+ (Everyone 10+)
- T (Teen)

- MA (Mature, 17+)

- Adults Only (18+)

- RP (Rating Pending, Rating Pending Likely Mature)

The ESRB also provides more than 30 different content descriptors to further explain why any game may have received any particular rating, such as "intense violence" or "crude humor".

ESRB – E for Everyone

ESRB – E10+ (Everyone 10 and over)

ESRB – T for Teen (13+)

ESRB – M for Mature (17+)

ESRB – AO (Adults Only, 18+)

ESRB – RP for Rating Pending

The ESRB isn't just a ratings system, mind you. The organization has created a suite of tools to help parents[2] make the right decisions around content in video games, including learning about parental controls, family gaming guides (which we, the authors, have both contributed to), and quick tips for being a "gaming parent." They even provide Spanish translations. All in all, the ESRB does a lot of the heavy lifting to help keep parents informed.

It was these regulatory building blocks that allowed games to experiment and become more of what they are today. The rating systems, whether that's through the ESRB (North America), PEGI (UK), ECOS (Japan), or USK (Germany), aren't perfect, but they're regularly updated to reflect the changes in the game industry.

Even when publishers make decisions about mechanics like loot boxes, microtransactions, online interactions, or downloadable content, these ratings boards evolve alongside the industry itself, ensuring that parents and guardians have the most up-to-date information possible when making decisions around what kinds of games to bring home.

Understanding "Escapism"

We all have preconceived notions of what video games are (and aren't) in relation to our children.

These days, our kids have access to technology that far outstrips what we grew up with, even those of us who had games and computers in our homes from the time we were small (like Amanda). It's a Star Trek kind of age out there with handheld computers that we call phones and the technological marvels that are tablets. The ubiquity of technology in every facet of our lives is marvelous and, for many of us, kind of terrifying at the same time.

It feels daunting, doesn't it? It can be. But the most important thing to remember about video games in particular is that even when it looks like your child is absolutely oblivious or obsessed (or both), there are some differences between positive escapism (which we love) and subversive escapism (which can be worrisome if left unchecked).

Positive escapism versus not so positive (subversive) escapism

We all need an escape from our daily lives. Whether that is escaping into a good book, a Netflix binge, or a video game. However, at what point does escapism go from a much needed respite to something more problematic? The difference between positive and non-so positive (or as researchers like to call it, subversive) escapism is relatively well-defined. Put simply, positive escapism allows us to "escape real life to reduce daily stress".[3] Subversive escapism is an "escape device [used] to avoid real life problems".

Positive escapism is essential for our mental health. We watch television, play sports, or read a great book to reduce stress on a regular basis. Video games, when used as a tool for positive escapism, can also be a fantastic portal to stress reduction (see mood management).

For Amanda, video games are a regular part of how she relaxes. Sometimes that's just sitting with my kids as they play something, playing a game with someone she loves, or indulging in her latest indie game obsession. She has a particular love of strategy games and roleplaying games (more on those genres below), especially when they're smooshed together in the same experience.

For Rachel, video games are also a regular part of how she relaxes. Nothing quite hits the spot like a farming simulator like Stardew Valley or unpacking and folding boxes in the indie sensation, Unpacking (which is a lot more fun than it sounds!). Of course, she loves a Netflix binge as much as the next person, but games are a regular part of her relaxation and leisure time.

It's the subversive escapism that we need to watch out for, especially as parents of older children and teenagers. If they're being bullied at school or there's an element of destabilization at home (moving, new school, divorce, death in the family, the ongoing trauma of the world at large, etc.), escaping into games can become a larger problem if it's left unexamined. This is the kind of escapism that many parents tend to believe that their children are dissolving into every single time that anyone plays a game, regardless of circumstance.

That's just not the case.

Subversive escapism looks a lot different than positive escapism and can include things such as:

- Neglecting personal health and hygiene
- Socially isolating from friends and family
- Avoiding or missing school and social obligations to play more games
- Starting to exhibit a strong preference for online rather than offline social interactions

Another way to think of positive versus subversive escapism is thinking about the behaviors as distraction or avoidance. Are games a distraction from the daily stresses of life? Are they something that is being engaged in for fun, to socialize with friends, and take a break from work and school? Or is it being used to avoid one's responsibilities, social interactions with others, and school and work obligations? If it is the latter, that may be cause for concern.

We all use escapism to distract ourselves from the pieces of our lives that are worrying us, just for a little while. A good book will distract us from exhaustion and overwhelm. Binging a great show distracts us from the scary things out in the real world. These are all reasonable ways to exist through overwhelm and stress.

On the other hand, avoidance as an expression of escapism can be crippling in the long-term. When we use escapism to avoid our problems (or our responsibilities), everything crumbles around us. When subversive escapism and avoidance exist in the same space, people tend to conflate the two with the spectre of "video game addiction."

Escapism versus addiction (Gaming Disorder)

Escapism isn't inherently bad, especially when it's used as a tool to destress and temporarily distract us from our troubles. We all do it to some extent. Escapism is also not analogous to "addiction".

Before moving on, it is worth taking a minute to discuss the differences between subversive escapism and avoidance, and "addiction" in a clinical sense.

When it comes to video games, there is a lot of discussion about addiction. As a parent, we're all concerned about which signs we should be looking for when it comes to drawing the line between potentially problematic and clinically addicted play.

In 2019, the WHO designated "Gaming Disorder" (i.e., video game addiction) for the new iteration of their "International Classification of Diseases" or ICD-11. According to the World Health Organization, the official criteria that need to be met for a diagnosis of Gaming Disorder are:

- Impaired control over gaming (e.g., onset, frequency, intensity, duration, termination, and context)

- Increasing priority given to gaming to the extent that gaming takes precedence over other life interests and daily activities

- Continuation or escalation of gaming despite the occurrence of negative consequences.

All of these symptoms must be present and this behavior pattern must be of sufficient severity to negatively impact personal, family, social, educational and/or other important areas of functioning. This behavior must be present for at least 12 months; however, the pattern of gaming behavior may be continuous (i.e., over 12 months in a row) or episodic and recurrent (i.e., spans of disordered gaming lasting for various amounts of time with moments of reprieve in between).

There has been a lot of debate within the research community about Gaming Disorder as a distinct clinical diagnosis, particularly in relation to the vagueness of the diagnostic criteria (in fact, this is one of the primary concerns from the scientific community). For example, if you replace the word "games" with another enjoyable activity that you often participate in – for example, dancing – you will likely find that you also meet the criteria for being "addicted" to that activity.

Many researchers also disagree with the WHO's decision to move forward with a formal classification of Gaming Disorder as there is no evidence to indicate that games themselves are the source of the problem. More importantly, the WHO has consistently failed to provide evidence that games are the problem. That is, there are no unique characteristics of video games themselves that have been identified as the source of physical, social, and psychological challenges for its players.

In fact, many researchers believe that the problematic use of games is more likely a coping mechanism for something else, such as depression or anxiety. This is important, as these distinctions would greatly impact intervention approaches. This is something to keep in mind when trying to understand why your child may be using games in a maladaptive way. Is it because they may be experiencing symptoms of depression? Do they have high social anxiety? These are all things to consider.

That said, if you are concerned about someone you know, you may want to seek professional help. The first step is to reach out to a qualified professional, preferably one who is culturally competent in and around games. This is key, as the use of games maladaptively could be due to another, primary challenge that should be the focus of intervention (depression, anxiety, etc.). In this sense, treating the "game play" may not be the most effective intervention and treatment plan. There are a ton of resources available online to help locate a culturally competent therapist, such as this directory from Take This.

So what's the takeaway here? There are people who use games problematically, and if that's the case, it's important to seek professional support. Games themselves aren't the problem per se, but can be used to accommodate or help cope with something else entirely... just like many, many other things that help us feel good and in control for periods of time.

However, we can rest assured knowing that our child playing their new favorite game ad nauseum over holiday break isn't necessarily a sign of problematic, disordered, or "addictive" play.

They're simply spending more time at the playground... the digital playground.

Media Attributions

- ESRB-E

- ESRB-E10

- ESRB-T

- ESRB-M

- ESRB-AO

- ESRB-RP

1. For more about the ESRB and its ratings visit www.esrb.org
2. For more detailed information about parental controls visit www.parentaltools.org
3. Bostan, B. (Ed.). (2020). Game User Experience And Player-Centered Design. Istanbul: Springer.

WELCOME TO THE DIGITAL PLAYGROUND

From simple single player games to elaborate and immersive virtual worlds, today's digital playgrounds have become a mainstay of our lives. While we all know the rules of the traditional playground, how do we, as parents and guardians, best prepare and care for our children in these digital spaces?

All of that preamble about the history of games, defining play itself, and even how legislation has helped shape the global game industry has been to prepare you for how to think about games in your child's life.

Think about your childhood for a moment. Think about the ways in which you played with your friends. Was it on a playground where the gravel was lava? Was it in a pool in the summertime, making up games about mermaids and dolphins? Was it playing baseball after school with the kids in your neighborhood? Was it playing road hockey in the crisp autumn air, yelling when a car came down the street?

These are all examples of play (which we've defined), the domain and true work of all children. These examples of play are also reflective of the time in which you grew up, whether you were a latchkey kid[1] or had a ton of parental presence yourself. Video games may or may not have been part of your childhood (though for those who had parents that loved video games themselves, welcome fellow nerds!)

For Rachel and Amanda, play in their childhoods also included the floor is lava, sticks as swords, and loosely organized sports with the neighborhood kids (hockey for Amanda, baseball for Rachel). However, it also included defeating Bowser in *Super Mario Bros.*, defeating Garland in the original *Final Fantasy*, humming the delightful chiptune sounds from *The Legend of Zelda*, and recreating the pranks of *Spy v. Spy* (Rachel still has a love/hate relationship with that game). Video games were one part of their childhood that was much loved by them but not an experience that was ubiquitously shared among their friends. (Consoles were still relatively rare in the mid-90s.)

Today, nearly every child plays video games of some kind. Video games are everywhere, including (but not limited to) word games on their parent's smartphone, home console(s), or games at a friend's house during a playdate. Video games are far more common, accessible, and integral to daily life as a form of play. To put the scope of video games into perspective, there are an estimated number or 3.24 billion players around the world[2]. In 2020, the Entertainment Software Association (ESA) reported that 75% of Americans have at least one video game player in their household[3].

Playgrounds, traditional and digital, are what scholars refer to as "third places". A third place is a space that is "neither for work no home but rather informal social life".[4] For adults, a third place could be a local pub or cafe. However, for children playgrounds have long been the space that fills this gap between structured work spaces (e.g., school) and leisure (e.g., organized sports, clubs). There are eight characteristics of a third place:

1. **Neutral ground**: spaces where individuals can come and go as they please

2. **Leveler**: a person's status in other venues (e.g., work, society at large) are not important. That is, participation is not reliant on any prerequisites.

3. **Conversation is the main activity**: Conversation is a core activity in the space

4. **Accessibility and accommodation**: third places must be easy to access

5. **The regulars**: There should be a regular "gang" of people who congregate there, that set the tone of conversation and general mood

6. **Low profile**: The spaces are not extravagant in a way that attracts a high volume of strangers or transient visitors

7. **The mood is playful**: There should be the sense of playfulness

8. **A home away from home**: One should feel rooted, have a sense of possession, regeneration, and being at ease when in a third place

If you look at this list and think about your childhood hangouts, you'll likely find that many of them fit the bill. Rachel's local arcade was one place that would meet these criteria as a "third place" where she spent much of her adolescence (though, for her brother it was probably the baseball diamond down the street from their house!).

Today, Video Games Are The New Third Place.

And for Amanda, her "third place" wasn't a physical location — it was on message boards, LiveJournal, and *Neopets* in the late-90s, early-2000s. She and her online friends talked endlessly about video games, makeup, anime, fantasy books, and digital art. These online forums were Amanda's safest spaces when she wasn't at school, at work, or out with friends. They're where she learned how to make pixel art and websites, where she learned how to be a good leader and nurturer online, and where she sharpened her skills as a writer.

Today, video games are the new third place. [5] Video games are the new playground for many of our children. They're not a separate, amorphous experience but rather an extension of the world that they inhabit every day. **They are spaces where children can meet up and play with their friends after school**; maybe hang out with an uncle that lives on the other side of the continent or the cousins that they see once a year at the lake during summer vacation. It is the new shared playground space, accessible nearly "anytime, anyplace, anywhere" where children can congregate, play, and socialize.

With all of this in mind, let's get to the practical bits of what our kids might be playing and how to help them navigate it all.

1. A "latchkey kid" refers to a child who is at home without adult supervision for some part of the day, especially after school until a parent comes home from work.
2. Statista (2021). Number of video gamers worldwide in 2021, by region. Retrieved from: https://www.statista.com/statistics/293304/number-video-gamers
3. https://www.theesa.com/resource/2020-essential-facts/
4. Oldenburg, R. (1999). The Great Good Place: Cafés, Coffee Shops, Community Centers, Beauty Parlors, General Stores, Bars, Hangouts, and How They Get You Through The Day. New York: Marlowe & Company
5. Steinkuehler, C. A., & Williams, D. (2006). Where everybody knows your (screen) name: Online games as "third places". Journal of computer-mediated communication, 11(4), 885-909.

TYPES OF GAMES

In some ways, all digital games are similar in that they are playful, interactive digital spaces. However, digital games can (and often do) vary greatly in terms of their content and the ways they are played. These differences are often discussed in terms of genre. The categorization of media into genres is common across media such as books and movies. Although, unlike traditional forms of media, game genres tend to be based on gameplay rather than more aesthetic features[1].

For example, a digital game where the player shoots at, or destroys a series of objects or opponents is typically classified under a "shooter" genre, regardless of the setting. Even though these two games couldn't be further apart in terms of content, *Call of Duty* and *Slime Rancher* are both considered shooters (though *Slime Rancher* is also considered a farming simulation game). *Call of Duty* games tend to be set in real-world settings (such as in *Call of Duty Modern Warfare*). *Slime Rancher* is an adorable simulation game where you corral and breed creatures called slimes, but you just happen to have a slime gun that is used to shoot enemies threatening your burgeoning ranch.

It's important to understand the different types of games, as defined by their genre, in order to better understand the content and gameplay within them. While no standardized system of genres currently exists, a brief outline of the most popular genres is presented below.

Action

The action genre are ones that focus on physical challenges and often require hand-eye coordination and quick reflexes. Shooter games are often considered a subgenre of action games.

Some examples of action games include *Uncharted* (Naughty Dog), *Call of Duty* (Activision), *God of War* (Sony Santa Monica), and the latest *Tomb Raider* trilogy (Crystal Dynamics & Eidos Montreal).

Fighting & Brawlers

Remember when we talked about the original *Mortal Kombat* bursting onto the scene in the '90s and helped change how video games are regulated globally. *Mortal Kombat* is a fighting game that's now 10+ titles deep after many, many years of success.

Fighting games feature two characters using special moves to kick and punch at one another until one character is victorious over the other. There are variations on this that allow for multiple fighters (tag-team) as well. Some examples include *Mortal Kombat* (Midway, NetherRealm Studios), *Soul Calibur* (Bandai Namco), and *King of Fighters* (SNK).

Brawlers are a bit different, in that they tend to feature a whole host of characters smacking each other around. If your kids are anything like ours, they've likely played a round of Super Smash Bros (Nintendo). Some games are side-scrolling brawlers like *Castle Crashers* (The Behemoth), *Scott Pilgrim vs. The World* (Ubisoft), and *Streets of Rage 4* (Dotemu).

Adventure

Adventure games were one of the first genres of video games ever created, starting with the text-based adventure *Colossal Cave Adventure* (1976). Adventure games are those with gameplay that don't require reflex challenges or action, but rather puzzle solving by interacting with people or the environment in a non-confrontational way.

Some examples of adventure games include *The Secret of Monkey Island* (Lucasarts), *King's Quest* (Sierra), *Night in the Woods* (Finji), *Everybody's Gone To The Rapture* (The Chinese Room), and *What Remains of Edith Finch* (Annapurna Interactive).

Action-Adventure

Action-adventure is a hybrid genre that combines the elements of both action and adventure. Typically, these games feature long-term obstacles with many smaller obstacles in the way (that require elements of action to overcome, like jumping from ledge to ledge). Action-adventure games tend to focus on item gathering and puzzle solving.

A few examples of action-adventure games include *Super Lucky's Tale* (Playful Studios), *Kirby and the Forgotten Land* (Nintendo), *Marvel's Spider-Man* (Insomniac Games), and *The Legend of Zelda: Breath of the Wild* (Nintendo).

Role-Playing

A role-playing game is one that requires the player to take on the role of a character to progress through a story. There are a number of different ways that a role-playing game can be structured. RPGs can sometimes employ a more action-oriented battle system (*The Witcher 3*, CD Projekt RED), a turn-based battle system (*Persona 5*, Sega Atlus), or an active battle system (*Final*

Fantasy 4, Square Enix). Whatever the choices on how the game's combat is implemented, the games themselves are all focused on taking on the role of a character (or set of characters) as they move through their story.

Offline role playing games, such as games from the Final Fantasy series (excluding *Final Fantasy 11*, *Final Fantasy 14*, and the *Crystal Chronicles* games), are exclusively single player endeavors.

Massively Multiplayer Online Role Playing Game

A notable subcategory of the role-playing genre is the massively multiplayer online role playing game or MMORPG. An MMORPG (or MMO for short) is a roleplaying game that's played with many other players in the same universe. There are opportunities to progress the story by yourself or with a party of players; you can engage in "dungeons" or "raids" to get better gear; and build communities through "guilds" and "companies."

Notable examples of games from this genre include *World of Warcraft* (Blizzard), *Black Desert Online* (Pearl Abyss), *Star Wars: The Old Republic* (Bioware/EA), *Warframe* (Digital Extremes), and *Final Fantasy 14* (Square Enix).

It's worth mentioning that *Destiny 2* (Bungie), while a first-person shooter, is very multiplayer oriented but is not actively considered an MMO. It just feels like one when you're playing it.

Sandbox

A sandbox game is one with gameplay elements that provide the player with a large degree of creativity to interact with the game environment with no predetermined goal or with a goal that the player sets for themselves.

One of the most popular sandbox games is *Minecraft* (Mojang).

Other notable examples include *Roblox* (Roblox Corporation), *Terraria* (Re-Logic), *Stardew Valley* (Concerned Ape), *Astroneer* (System Era Softworks), *Valheim* (Iron Gate), *No Man's Sky* (Hello Games), and *Kerbal Space Program* (Squad, Private Division).

Shooter

Shooter games are those that involve shooting at or destroying a series of objects or opponents. Shooter games can be played from either a first-person (i.e., gameplay is viewed through the eyes of the player) or third-person (i.e., gameplay is viewed from behind or a birds-eye) perspective. This is what is being referred to when you hear the terms "first person shooter (FPS)" or "third-person shooter (TPS).

Notable examples of games from this genre include *Call of Duty* (Activision), *Fortnite* (Epic Games), *Apex Legends* (Respawn), *Mass Effect* (Bioware), *Gears of War* (The Coalition, Xbox Game Studios), *The Division* (Ubisoft), and *BioShock* (Irrational Games).

Simulation

Simulation games are those that simulate real-world activities. This can be a single task such as flying (e.g., *Microsoft Flight Simulator*) or more complex tasks such as the simulation of civilizations (e.g., *Civilization* series of games) or families (e.g., *The Sims*).

Strategy

The strategy genre refers to games that emphasize the use of strategy as opposed to fast action or quick reflexes. Strategy games can be played in either "real time" (i.e., gameplay between the user and competitor takes place in real time) or "turn-based" (i.e., each player gets an unlimited amount of time to make a certain number of decisions that constitutes their turn). This is what is referred to when you hear the terms "real-time strategy" (RTS) and "turn-based strategy" (TBS) games.

Some noteworthy examples of strategy games include *Starcraft* (Blizzard), *Star Renegades* (Raw Fury), *Stellaris* (Paradox Interactive), *Slay the Spire* (Mega Crit Games, and *Age of Empires* (Xbox Game Studios).

Multiplayer Online Battle Arena (MOBA)

A notable sub-genre of strategy games is the multiplayer online battle area or MOBA. These games feature three lanes of play, where players need to strategize to maximize their level, damage, and effectiveness against the other team. The goal is to destroy the other team's towers, defenses, and eventually their base through superior tactics.

Notable MOBAs include *League of Legends* (Riot Games), *DOTA 2* (Valve), *Smite* (Hi Rez Studios), *Heroes of the Storm* (Blizzard), *Paladins* (Hi Rez Studios), and *VainGlory* (Super Evil Megacorp).

Sports

Sports games are those that are adaptations of existing sports (e.g., football, tennis) or variations of them. There are simulation games and arcade games. Simulation sports games can be deeply complex and require a lot of work to become proficient at them. Arcade sports games are more approachable and appropriate for fans of the sport that don't want to get too bogged down in rules.

Sports simulation games are ubiquitous but some of the most popular franchises are developed and published by EA (FIFA, NHL, Madden NFL, PGA, racing), 2K Games (NBA, WWE), and Sony (MLB).

Arcade sports games are more along the lines of *NBA Jam*

(Acclaim   Entertainment   &   Midway   Games),   *WWE   2K Battlegrounds* (2K Games), *Forza Horizon 5* (Xbox Game Studios), and *Blood Bowl* (Cyanide).

Party

Party games are those designed for many players and are often used as forms of entertainment at social gatherings. One of the most popular series is the *Jackbox Party Pack* (Jackbox Games), which is currently in its 8th installment.

Puzzle

While many games across genres use puzzles in their gameplay, to be considered in the puzzle genre, problem solving must be the primary gameplay activity. This can include logic puzzles, pattern recognition, or word completion. Notable examples in this genre include *Wordle* (The New York Times), *Tetris* (Alexey Pajitnov), and *Portal* (Valve).

1. Apperley, T. H. (2006). Genre and game studies: Toward a critical approach to video game genres. Simulation & gaming, 37(1), 6-23

OFFLINE VS. ONLINE

Long gone is the trope of the isolated, socially inept game player sitting in a basement playing games by themselves (though, that stereotype was never actually rooted in reality[1], but that's a topic for a different day).

In the years leading up to the rise of social media and VoIP (voice over IP, such as Skype and Zoom), the lines between online and offline were already starting to become blurry. From where we're sitting in 2022, the lines don't exist anymore. Online is ubiquitous, it's everywhere and in everything from our phones to our fridges. Or as Rachel likes to say, the internet is accessible nearly "anytime, anyplace, and anywhere."

What this means for video games is a little bit different than what it means when we go on "social media breaks" for our mental health. When we think about online games, we tend to think of games like *World of Warcraft* or *Roblox* or even private *Minecraft* servers. In actuality, online games are in everything from your single player blockbusters on PlayStation to *Animal Crossing* on Nintendo Switch or even a tiny little indie game that you play on your phone.

Today, being always online is just a part of how we own and play games. As the game industry moves more and more towards a digital-only future, servers need to check for game licenses to see if you own the game you're trying to play and the platform's operating system (on Xbox, Nintendo, or PlayStation) needs to make sure that your version of the game is up-to-date. Both of these tasks require the internet.

Online is everywhere, especially in games. Yes, even single player games are connected to other players and networks through leaderboards and shared chat systems.

Now it is important to note that there is a difference between a game being "always online" to check for updates and licenses and the game itself requiring a consistent connection to a game's servers and online players. One of these things — licenses and updates — is just a normal part of owning a video game. The other is where parental controls come in. On almost every platform that you can play a video game on, there are ways to control how a game interacts with your device and how your child interacts with that game.

On mobile devices, there are ways to not only set screen-time limits but to also ensure that games aren't collecting location data or user information without your permission as a parent. Thanks to the Child Online Privacy Protection Act of 1998, websites and online services geared towards children have to follow certain rules to ensure a child's privacy is protected. It's the reason why we have age gates on making online accounts for everything from forums to Facebook.

CNET has a useful guide[2] on the things that you can do on iOS to ensure better safety on any Apple mobile device. Family Zone details[3] how to turn off location data sharing on Android. Finally, USA Today has some great tips[4] on how to make the most of privacy settings on both platforms.

Online communication can also be curtailed on console platforms through parental controls. PlayStation allows parents to set limits on everything from who the child can communicate with to how much money they're allowed to spend in the PlayStation digital store. Xbox's is even more robust, as it links into Windows accounts. While you're setting limits for your child on Xbox, you can set them for Windows as well.

The ESRB has some great guides[5] on how to accomplish all of this on each of the current generation (Nintendo Switch, PlayStation 5, and Xbox Series) consoles and the last generation (PlayStation 4 and Xbox One) consoles, as well as Windows.

1. Kowert, R., Festl, R., & Quandt, T. (2014). Unpopular, overweight, and socially inept: Reconsidering the stereotype of online gamers. Cyberpsychology, Behavior, and Social Networking, 17(3), 141-146.

2. Elliott, M. (2019, Jan 10). 7 parental controls you can use right now on your kid's iPhone. CNET. Retrieved from https://www.cnet.com/tech/mobile/parental-controls-you-can-use-right-now-on-your-kids-iphone/

3. https://docs.familyzone.com/help/turn-off-location-tracking-android

4. Komando, K. (2019, Feb 14). How to stop your smartphone from tracking your every move, sharing data and sending ads. USA Today. Retrieved from https://www.usatoday.com/story/tech/columnist/komando/2019/02/14/your-smartphone-tracking-you-how-stop-sharing-data-ads/2839642002/

5. https://www.esrb.org/tools-for-parents/parental-controls/

WHY OUR KIDS NEED DIGITAL PLAYGROUNDS

Play has always been a valued use of time for children. However, digital play is often seen as a "sub-par" or "lesser" valued form of play. Since the COVID-19 pandemic began, it has become crystal clear that digital playgrounds are not "less than" but a vital component of play in our children's lives.

Our children had already been using video games as a socialization tool for quite some time before they lost access to their friends for over a year. During the lockdowns, children had no choice but to step into online worlds to see their friends. They had, and still have, virtual playdates in everything from *Fortnite* to *Minecraft*. They kept their social skills sharp through spending time learning to communicate digitally during a *Fortnite* match, instead of only talking in person. They worked on leadership skills while building digital microcosms of society with economic structures, law enforcement, and even civic systems in *Minecraft*. During this time, the little ones even brushed up on their social skills, simple mathematics, and developed a new understanding of the stock (er, turnip) market through *Animal Crossing*.

Kids need spaces where they feel safe, even if those spaces are in video games.

We inhabit a world where children are no longer limited to seeing each other at the park after school or on the weekends. They can come home, do their homework, and then log into Zoom (an old nemesis from distance learning during 2020-21) to play some Minecraft with their best friends. They laugh, shout, collaborate, disagree (sometimes mightily), roughhouse, celebrate victories, and create entire worlds to play in.

The only difference between "playing house" and "playing *Minecraft*" is in the medium of play, rather than play itself.

Jordan Shapiro, author of The New Childhood, shared a story of how he learned to use the telephone when he was a kid and how play showed him how to have fun using a phone through prank phone calls. Kids are doing this with the technology of today, too. They're learning the rules of how to use these systems, whether that's Facebook Messenger for Kids or texting or even Zoom calls, through their most important work as children: playing.

Our world is hyper-connected through text messages, emails, Slack, and social media. If our children are to survive (and thrive) in this global network of fast-moving communication and information, they need digital playgrounds to be safe spaces to experiment, express themselves, and connect with their peers.

The New Childhood reminds us that "our children are playing without responsible mentorship"[1] because too many parents are afraid of this digital landscape. And without that guidance, without best practices being presented by parents, guardians, and mentors, children are unsupported and will fill in the blanks either by watching YouTube or, more likely, watching their peers who have similar problems.

It's Our Job As Parents And Guardians To Get Our Hands Dirty In The Voxel Sandbox And Learn To Play Together.

1. Shapiro, J. (2018). The New Childhood: Raising kids to thrive in a connected world. New York: Little, Brown Spark.

THE NEW RULES OF THE PLAYGROUND

While the digital spaces of the 21st century may be the new playground, the rules need to evolve to fit the spaces. For instance, parents may be less inclined to encourage their children to play with strangers, even if said strangers might be other children, on the digital playground. We're both of a similar mind, to be honest. So how do we navigate these new spaces and what are the rules?

Rachel and Amanda have children from a wide range of ages, including a toddler and a college student. The conversations that they've had with each of their children have been slightly different depending on age and maturity, but each chat started off with meeting the kids where they are. Rachel's conversations with her young children are much different than the conversations that Amanda has with her teenagers and older children.

The guiding light with any kind of ruleset that you put in place around video games and interactive content is to be willing to evolve alongside your child's maturity, age, and understanding of the world at large. As children grow, they'll push back on limits. It's what they do. As long as you're willing to grow your understanding of gaming (which you're already doing!), you'll continue to be able to meet them where they are.

And these books will help you along the way.

The advice that follows isn't prescriptive and shouldn't be considered as such. Based on Rachel's research and the duo's many years of experience as parents and gamers themselves, what follows is how we've approached these conversations and our recommendations.

Time Limits

The most important thing to keep in mind when imposing time limits is the context of the limits. Limits may need to be stricter during the school year when your child needs ample time to complete schoolwork and other after-school commitments (sports, work, etc.). During holidays, these limits may become looser as your child has more leisure time. While generally speaking, time limits increase with age, sometimes even children of the same age may need different restrictions on time.

How Amanda has approached limitations on screen time between children of similar ages (since she has a cluster of kids around the same age) is to be honest with each of them about what she's observed as their own emotional limitations.

For instance, one of her children is neurodivergent and requires strict boundaries and limits in order to stay safe emotionally. Once they reach a certain threshold of time during the course of a day, they're less able to regulate their emotions and become prone to irritability. So, the hard limits that Amanda and her co-parents impress on them is to keep them safe. The other younger children have fewer rigid rules around time the vast majority of the time (as they're now self-regulating), but those rules change when moods become affected by too much time-consuming content and not enough time making.

Rating systems such as the ESRB help to provide parents with information about the content of a game.

That said, whether or not something is appropriate for your child is a different story. Some children are perfectly comfortable engaging in explicit content before they're eighteen, whereas others may not be.

For Rachel's children, anything even remotely scary does not go over well in her household so she refrains from engaging in that kind of media, regardless of the age rating. For Amanda's, hyperviolence makes each of her children very uncomfortable so they refrain from the vast majority of first-person shooters and all horror games. As our children grow, their needs and interests will change. Amanda's youngest is her "creepy darling" (a most loving moniker, rest assured) and as she gets older, she will likely become a horror game aficionado like her mother.

For content, be sure you are informing yourself as a parent with all the tools and information at hand: age ratings, content descriptors, short descriptions of the gameplay/plot, and live playthroughs on services such as YouTube or Twitch (www.twitch.tv). There has never been more accessibility to the information about the kinds of games we play as we have today, and we should be taking advantage of that to make sure we are as well informed as we can about the content of media our children are consuming (we tend do it for movies and television, why not games?).

Creating house rules should be something done collaboratively between parents and children. When children help create the rules they feel a sense of ownership and are more likely to abide by them as they are something they created together rather than something imposed upon them from the outside.

Personal Limits

No two children are exactly the same and therefore every single one of our kids will have different needs and limits on time and content. These limits will continue to morph and change as the child gets older, matures, and learns how to self-regulate their own balance between responsibilities and leisure.

The goal is self-regulation, of course. We can't watch over our children as they head off to college or into the workforce. One day they will grow up and we will have let them make their own mistakes, just like our parents had to. The ultimate goal of any of these conversations is to ensure that they can make good decisions around video games (with regards to content and time spent) when we stop keeping such a close eye on them.

Goodness knows that Amanda lost a day or two here and there playing marathon Civilization sessions, which wasn't great decision-making on her part, but she survived. And Rachel definitely spent more days than she'd like to admit playing World of Warcraft. Even still, she always managed to continue to meet her responsibilities for work and school. The takeaway here is that everyone's limit is different.

All children want to be autonomous, so the best thing that we can do is be a firmer guiding hand when they're young and loosen things up as they get older. As Amanda and Rachel both say in their households, the best way that we stay connected to one another is to keep those communication lines open. Our kids won't tell us everything that happens, whether that's on the digital playground or in their peer relationships, but by establishing trust early on, we can ensure that they know that we're always here.

CONCLUDING THOUGHTS

Digital games have long been considered as "separate" or "other than" traditional forms of play. However, digital games are simply a new form of the classic forms of play we've championed as part of normal development for centuries. Our hope is that the information within this book will help bring digital games away from topics of conflict, and towards topics of conversation. With the right tools and safeguards at hand, parents can feel confident navigating these new digital playgrounds.

Now that you have the building blocks for understanding video games in context, the next books in our series will go even deeper into each of these topics. The next book in the Digital Playgrounds series will discuss all the ways in which video games can be used for good (connection, education, and play) and, if left unexamined and unexplored, can also be used for not-so-good (aggression, addiction, and toxic gamer cultures).

We hope that you'll come along with us.

ABOUT THE ETC PRESS

The ETC Press was founded in 2005 under the direction of Dr. Drew Davidson, the Director of Carnegie Mellon University's Entertainment Technology Center (ETC), as an open access, digital-first publishing house.

What does all that mean?

The ETC Press publishes three types of work:peer-reviewed work (research-based books, textbooks, academic journals, conference proceedings), general audience work (trade nonfiction, singles, Well Played singles), and research and white papers

The common tie for all of these is a focus on issues related to entertainment technologies as they are applied across a variety of fields.

Our authors come from a range of backgrounds. Some are traditional academics. Some are practitioners. And some work in between. What ties them all together is their ability to write about the impact of emerging technologies and its significance in society.

To distinguish our books, the ETC Press has five imprints:

- **ETC Press:** our traditional academic and peer-reviewed publications;

- **ETC Press: Single:** our short "why it matters" books that are roughly 8,000-25,000 words;

- **ETC Press: Signature:** our special projects, trade books, and other curated works that exemplify the best work being done;

- **ETC Press: Report:** our white papers and reports produced by practitioners or academic researchers working in conjunction with partners; and

- **ETC Press: Student:** our work with undergraduate and graduate students

In keeping with that mission, the ETC Press uses emerging technologies to design all of our books and Lulu, an on-demand publisher, to distribute our e-books and print books through all the major retail chains, such as Amazon, Barnes & Noble, Kobo, and Apple, and we work with The Game Crafter to produce tabletop games.

We don't carry an inventory ourselves. Instead, each print book is created when somebody buys a copy.

Since the ETC Press is an open-access publisher, every book, journal, and proceeding is available as a free download. We're most interested in the sharing and spreading of ideas. We also have an agreement with the Association for Computing Machinery (ACM) to list ETC Press publications in the ACM Digital Library.

Authors retain ownership of their intellectual property. We release all of our books, journals, and proceedings under one of two Creative Commons licenses:

- **Attribution-NoDerivativeWorks-NonCommercial:** This license allows for published works to remain intact, but versions can be created; or

- **Attribution-NonCommercial-ShareAlike:** This license allows for authors to retain editorial control of their creations while also encouraging readers to collaboratively rewrite content.

This is definitely an experiment in the notion of publishing, and we invite people to participate. We are exploring what it means to "publish" across multiple media and multiple versions. We believe this is the future of publication, bridging virtual and physical media with fluid versions of publications as well as enabling the creative blurring of what constitutes reading and writing.

THE AUTHORS

Authors

Amanda Farough
http://www.amandafarough.com
http://www.twitter.com/
amandafarough

Amanda Farough has been many things in her life — business analyst, consultant, game journalist, speaker, entrepreneur, and writer. Over the course of her work as an analyst and journalist, she's focused on the business side of how video games are made (www.virtualeconcast.com) and on how parents can navigate the world of games without being gamers themselves. Amanda has four kids and when she's not writing, streaming (www.twitch.tv/readyplayermama), or consulting on video games, she's hanging out with them.

Rachel Kowert, PhD
http://www.rkowert.com
http://www.twitter.com/DrKowert

Rachel Kowert, Ph.D is a research psychologist and the Research Director of Take This. She is a world-renowned researcher on the uses and effects of digital games, including their impact on physical, social, and psychological well-being. An award-winning author, she has published a variety of books and scientific articles relating to the psychology of games and, more recently, the relationship between games and mental health specifically. She also serves as the editor of the Routledge Debates in Media Studies series and the upcoming ETC press series Psychology of Pop Culture. Recently, she founded her YouTube channel Psychgeist, which serves to bridge the gap between moral panic and scientific knowledge on a variety of psychology and game-related topics. In 2021, Dr. Kowert was chosen as a member of The Game Awards Future Class, representing the best and brightest of the future of video games. Dr. Kowert has been featured in various media outlets, including NPR, the Washington Post, and the Wall Street Journal. To learn more about Rachel and her work, visit www.rkowert.com.

Ingram Content Group UK Ltd.
Milton Keynes UK
UKHW052228050623
422930UK00001B/9